Workbook

UMI

God's Vision or Television?

How Television Influences What We Believe

CARL JEFFREY WRIGHT

Urban Ministries, Inc.
The African American Christian Publishing & Communications Co.

Writer: C. Jeffrey Wright

Publisher
Urban Ministries, Inc.
P.O. Box 436987
Chicago, IL 60643-6897
1-800-860-8642

First Edition
First Printing
ISBN: 0-940955-92-X

Table of Contents

PREFACE

GOD'S VISION OR TELEVISION? STUDENT WORKBOOK

This student workbook is to be used in conjunction with the book, *God's Vision or Television?* edited by Carl Jeffrey Wright. It is designed to help the reader apply principles learned in the book to real-life situations. The workbook can be used in a variety of Christian Education settings, including weekday Bible studies, retreats, Vacation Bible School courses, and Christian Education Congresses. It can also be used for individual, family, or church Bible study situations.

The chapters begin with a case study that describes a situation related to the issues in the respective chapters in the book. Except in the two cases that recount actual historical events, all names and persons used in these cases are completely fictitious. After each case study there is a series of questions that allows the reader to explore how passages from the Bible apply to the case.

The Ministry Application exercise allows the participant to either create or develop a related church-based ministry. The forms provided for each related ministry can be transferred to overhead transparencies to facilitate group participation.

The Personal Application exercises encourage each participant to take an inward look at their own struggles with each topic being considered. These questions can be used as take home assignments as well as in daily devotions.

CHAPTER ONE

TELEVISION—Is What You See Really What You Get?

CASE STUDY

In 2003, Howard Dean was one of the earliest candidates to launch a bid for presidency of the United States. Virtually unknown around the nation, it would have seemed unlikely that this governor from Vermont, one of the smallest and least populous states, had any prospects for winning. Soon things changed, or at least they appeared to. Television and other media became very interested in Mr. Dean. His views against the war in Iraq were strong, and he proposed repealing tax cuts that the current administration had instituted. Dean was also raising a lot of money over the Internet. His Internet fund-raising drew millions of dollars and even more television coverage.

In 2004, television news coverage of the Dean candidacy continued to increase as the first primary election was rapidly approaching. Televised debates featuring the seven other candidates ended with news commentators discussing what Howard Dean had said or how other candidates attacked Dean's positions. Dean was often declared the front-runner by the press and seemed to be able to do no wrong. But in one interview, he revealed his ignorance of the Bible by stating that an Old Testament book, Job, was his favorite New Testament text. Though there was some television criticism, it did not last long; and soon Dean was declared "the candidate to beat" by most television stations.

Finally, the first primary election took place. All the television news was focused on how Dean would do. Dean lost, badly. Within a few weeks, several other state primary elections took place. Dean lost every one of them. Howard Dean made the decision to withdraw, and his presidential campaign was dead. However, he did win the primary election in his home state of Vermont after he withdrew.

BIBLE APPLICATION EXERCISES
Jesus, God's Promised Son

1. Old Testament Prophecy

In film or television, a reference about a future event in the story is called "foreshadowing." What do the following Scriptures foreshadow (prophesy) about the Messiah?

a. Genesis 3:15

____

____

b. Isaiah 9:6–7; Psalm 16:10

c. Isaiah 7:14

d. Zechariah 11:12–13

e. Psalm 22:15–18

f. Using the Scriptures referenced above, describe how the Bible gives proof that Jesus was the Messiah.

2. New Testament Prophetic Fulfillment

How does Christ show the connection between Old Testament teachings and His ministry in the following Scriptures?

a. Matthew 1:22–23

b. John 3:14 (Numbers 21:8–9)

c. Matthew 11:13–14

d. Matthew 12:40–41

e. John 19:23–36

f. How did Jesus use the Scriptures in His ministry, and what was His purpose in doing so?

3. Biblical Truth—What Does the Bible Define as Truth?

What does the Bible say about truth in the following Scriptures?

a. John 17:17

b. Proverbs 12:19

c. John 1:1–2, 14

d. John 14:6

e. John 4:24

f. How will truth guide believers today? How will they differ from the world (John 14:15–17)?

4. The Enemy of Truth

What are the enemy's plans to use the media to keep people in bondage and how have we succumbed to them?

a. 2 Corinthians 4:4

b. Romans 1:18–21

c. John 8:44

d. 2 Corinthians 10:5; James 3:16

e. Acts 7:51

f. What approaches should the believer use to avoid deception in the media?

5. The Response of the Christian

What should be the Christian's response to news and information on television?

a. 2 Corinthians 13:8; Ephesians 6:14

b. 2 Timothy 2:15

c. Acts 17:10–11

d. Acts 20:20–21

e. Ephesians 4:15

f. Apply the Scriptures above to a current news story of your choosing and develop a Christian response to the story.

6. Ministry Application

Consider the plan outlined below or develop a plan for a weekly or monthly discussion group to address current events, news, or media events in light of Scripture.

Objective

Media Sources to be Used *(television programs, news magazines, radio reports, Internet stories)*

Selection Process for Topic to be Discussed

Participant Preparation

Scripture Application

7. Personal Application

Allow yourself time to carefully reflect on the following questions.

How can you guard your faith from falsehood?

How has television influenced what you believe?

Besides watching television, what can you do to get the news and information you need to make decisions?

Make a personal commitment to examine at least one other source before you repeat a story that you heard on television.

CHAPTER TWO

TELEVISION—God's Promises and TV's Promises

CASE STUDY

John and Jean grew up in the same neighborhood in Detroit and were married right after high school. He was a city bus driver, and she had a front desk job working at a major new downtown hotel. After a stressful day at work, John liked to come home and unwind in front of the TV. Sometimes he would eat dinner in front of the TV as well. They had no children and spent a lot of time on their relationship. As John put it to the marriage ministry group he led at their church, "You have to work harder on your marriage than you do your job." For Jean this meant lots of gifts and a regular date night out each week with John.

When John decided he needed a new sport utility vehicle in addition to their two-year-old sports car, Jean understood her husband's feelings. They were thinking about starting a family and they could use the extra room. John drove for a living and even though the truck they wanted was expensive, she felt he knew the best SUV to buy. The couple worked together the day before delivery to remove the exercise equipment and clean out the other stuff in the garage so there would be space to park both cars. Shortly after they got the new SUV, they began to fall behind on their many credit card bills. Even worse, the SUV was a gas guzzler; they were paying twice as much for gas, and John was reminded of this every time he filled up. They had not figured that the costs of owning and operating an SUV would be this much.

BIBLE APPLICATION EXERCISES
God Keeps His Promise

1. The Nature of God's Promises

Describe the nature of God's promises according to the following Scriptures.

a. 2 Samuel 22:31

____

b. Psalm 12:6

____

c. Psalm 18:30

d. Psalm 91:4

e. Isaiah 45:19

f. Compare the promises of God to the promises made by the sellers of products and services being advertised on television. What are some key differences?

2. God's Promises for Those Who Keep His Commands

What do the following Scriptures teach about the promises God makes to those who keep His commands?

a. 1 Kings 8:23

b. Daniel 9:4

c. Romans 15:4

d. 2 Peter 1:4–5

e. Deuteronomy 4:31

f. What are some of the benefits of keeping the commands of God?

3. Keeping Your Promises

What do the following Scriptures teach about keeping your promises?

a. 1 Samuel 20:23

b. Psalm 116:14

c. Ecclesiastes 5:2

d. Ecclesiastes 5:4

e. Romans 3:3

f. An unpaid bill is a broken promise. What can we learn from these Scriptures to help avoid becoming mired down in debt and too many financial commitments?

4. The Enemy of God's Promises

What do these Scriptures reveal about the ways of the enemy and those who do not receive the promises of God?

a. Genesis 3:1–5

b. Matthew 4:3, 6, 9

c. 1 Peter 5:8

d. Hebrews 3:18–19

e. Hebrews 6:12

f. How can the Scriptures above be used to avoid the pitfalls of deceptive advertising on television and in other media?

5. The False Promises of the Enemy

Describe what these Scriptures tell us about the enemy's false promises and deceit.

a. Ephesians 4:14

b. 2 Timothy 4:3–4

c. Colossians 2:8

d. 2 Thessalonians 2:9–10

e. 1 John 4:1

f. What can we summarize about the deception of Satan and the programming of television? What is the message for the believer?

6. Ministry Application

Develop a ministry plan for a clothing bank.

Focus Scripture

Objectives

Strategies (How we will accomplish our objectives.)

Community Resources (What groups are available to help in distribution or identification of those in need?)

Church Resources (What resources will the church need to provide for volunteers for this ministry?)

Space

Communication

Training

Literature/Publicity Items

Other

Alternative Ministry Application

Develop a "promise ring" ceremony for the young people of your church who commit to remain abstinent until marriage. Include the significance of promises we make before God, the biblical mandate for purity, and the importance of a ring or other symbol of the commitment. Use the Scriptures to reinforce this commitment or promise, and contrast it to the deceptions about this subject shown on television.

7. Personal Application

Make a commitment to give to the poor everything you have that you do not need. Consider clothing, household items, toys, games, appliances, and furniture. Make a list of the items and set a definite time to give these things away.

Turn off the shopping channel. If you frequently or occasionally watch television shopping channels, make a commitment to stop. If you do not watch shopping channels, tune in for a half hour and make a list of the methods used to entice viewers to buy. Commit to hold yourself above these temptations.

Allow yourself time to carefully reflect on the following questions.

What promises have you broken that you need to make good on?

Do you owe someone money?

Do you need to return borrowed items?

Do you pay your tithes?

Are there broken or unfulfilled promises to your spouse?

Are there broken or unfulfilled promises to your kids?

Are there broken or unfulfilled promises at your job?

CHAPTER THREE

TELEVISION—Miracles and Ministry

CASE STUDY

Reverend Charles always felt his ministry would do better if it was televised. Many local churches were on television and the costs seemed reasonable. The television station sales rep explained that by printing a prayer hotline number at the bottom of the screen, they could get names and addresses when people called in and their future contributions would more than pay for this television ministry.

The church broadcasts began and the entire congregation was dressed their best for the first program. Soon the contributions began to come in from television viewers. Reverend Charles decided to write a book on healing and offer it in exchange for monetary contributions from the television viewers. As more offerings came in, the church was remodeled, new equipment was purchased, and the television program was expanded from 30 minutes to an hour.

Although the budget of the church increased significantly from this effort, there was little change in the missions giving or community outreach of the church. The church budget reached one million dollars a year, but less than five percent was spent on non-television outreach activities. Many felt that this was the best-equipped church they had ever attended, though.

BIBLE APPLICATION EXERCISES
The Life/Ministry of Jesus

1. Old Testament Miracles of Healing

Summarize the healing miracles that took place in the following passages of Scripture.

a. 1 Kings 17:17–24

____

____

b. 2 Kings 5:1–14

____

____

c. Job 1:13–2:7; 42:10–12

d. Daniel 4:28–36

e. Isaiah 38:1–6

f. What do these Scriptures teach about the relationship between prayer, obedience, and healing?

2. New Testament Miracles of Healing

Summarize the healing miracles that took place in the following passages of Scripture.

a. Matthew 8:1–4

b. Matthew 9:27–31

c. Mark 7:31–37

d. John 5:1–9

e. Matthew 8:14–15

f. In what ways do these healing miracles demonstrate the healing power of Jesus?

3. Jesus Confronts the Pharisees' Objections about Healing

a. In Matthew 12:9–14, why did the Pharisees seek to destroy Jesus?

b. In Matthew 9:32–34, what power did the Pharisees accuse Jesus of using to heal?

c. How did Jesus address the Pharisees' arguments about the source of His healing power (Matthew 12:22–32)?

d. What dilemma did the Pharisees face in their investigation of Jesus' healing of the blind man in John 9:13–16?

e. How did Jesus describe the Pharisees in John 9:39–41?

f. Based on the above passages, what observations can we make about the religious leaders of Jesus' day and those of today?

4. Will Everyone Be Healed?

a. What did David do in response to the illness of his infant son (2 Samuel 12:15–23)?

b. What was David's response at the death of the child, and how did he comfort himself?

c. What reason did Jesus give for the inability of the disciples to heal the child in Matthew 17:14–21?

d. What was Paul's explanation for some deaths and illness among Christians in 1 Corinthians 11:27-32?

e. What is the formula for healing provided in James 5:13-15?

f. What should the church's response to illness be today?

5. Healing and Television Ministries

(Refer to Reverend Charles' case study at the beginning of this chapter.)

a. What were some good reasons for Reverend Charles' ministry to be televised?

b. How could Reverend Charles' book on healing have been used in his television ministry? What biblical support can you provide for your position?

c. What are your feelings about the use of the money raised from the television ministry of Reverend Charles' church? Why?

d. Is television outreach the same as outreach in the local community? Why or why not?

e. What other ways could Reverend Charles' church have demonstrated the power of God in their ministry?

f. Discuss the reasons for or against having special church healing services.

6. Ministry Application

How can you transform your ministry to reflect more of the power of God? Make a plan.

7. Personal Application

Define a list of standards for choosing which television ministries you will watch.

CHAPTER FOUR

TELEVISION—Salvation and Love

CASE STUDY

Andrette was "late"—two months late. She could not believe that her first time, onetime encounter with Justin could have this result. "God surely could have given me a break," she thought. After all, she had rarely missed Sunday School, church service, or Bible study in her entire 16 years of life. Justin's response to her phone call was just as incredulous. How could God allow the youth pastor's son, the head of the junior usher board, to get in this kind of situation? Wasn't his consistent prayer life as a 17-year-old enough to protect him from a mistake like this? They had danced the MTV-inspired routines after school countless times before without getting carried away like they did that time.

Justin went over the event in his mind again and again. Practicing the Super Bowl halftime hip-hop dance routine with Andrette after school was supposed to prepare him for the perfect performance at their high school's annual talent festival. He needed to win that contest so he could become a shoo-in for student body president. This would be the crowning achievement to his high school career. Now all he could think of was his conversation with his Dad about seeing who he would meet in college before deciding Andrette was "the one." But he agreed with Andrette that when all four parents returned from the church marriage retreat this weekend, they had to tell them about their coming grandchild.

BIBLE APPLICATION EXERCISES
God's Love Manifested in Our Salvation

1. The Bible's Definition of Love

a. What are the similarities and the differences between the situation that Justin faced and those that Joseph faced in Genesis 39:6–18?

____

____

b. How does the love of Jonathan and David described in 1 Samuel 20:1–17 compare to the love of Andrette and Justin?

____

c. Contrast the situation of David in 2 Samuel 11 with Justin's situation. What principles can be drawn from the two instances?

d. What are the characteristics of love defined in 1 Corinthians 13?

e. How did Jesus illustrate God's love in John 3:16?

f. What would you define as love? How could Justin and Andrette know love?

2. The Role of Parental Love

a. What role did Rebekah and Isaac play in the selection of a mate for their son (Genesis 27:46–28:2; 29:1–18)?

b. In Ruth 3:1–4, how did Naomi express concern for the remarriage of her daughter-in-law Ruth?

c. How should Justin and Andrette's parents respond to the news they are going to get from their children?

d. Is providing love-relationship training a responsibility of parents? Give scriptural authority for your answer.

e. What kind of support should the parents provide for their teen parents in the case study?

f. In what ways might the parents have contributed to the situation faced by Justin and Andrette?

3. Love and Power

a. What does Genesis 11:1–9 teach about the potential of man's love of power?

b. What is the result of the quest for the power equal to that of God (Isaiah 14:12–15)?

c. How might Justin's desire to become student body president have affected his relationship?

d. What are the outcomes of manipulation in the relationship between Jezebel and Ahab in 1 Kings 21?

e. How was Jesus tempted with an offer of great power (Matthew 4:8–9)?

f. How can the lessons from the previous verses be applied to the situation of Justin and Andrette? What should be their primary focus?

4. Love Versus Lust

a. What are the three areas of temptation described by John in 1 John 2:16, and how were they presented to Jesus in Matthew 4?

b. How was Justin tempted, and what should have been his response to temptation?

c. How might Justin have been better prepared than Andrette to overcome lust and temptation? What could have made him more susceptible to temptation?

d. What does Jesus' teaching in Matthew 5:27–28 suggest about Justin's encounters with Andrette?

e. How does Psalm 101:3 provide a prescription against lust?

f. According to the Scriptures above, how can parents help their children avoid the lusts of the flesh and the consequences?

5. The Love of God

a. Justin and Andrette have fallen short of God's standard and disappointed their parents. The consequences of their behavior are lifelong. How does God respond to them?

b. How do we know that forgiveness is available to the teens?

c. What facts in the case suggest that Justin and Andrette may have been bargaining for God's love? Why is this futile?

d. If Justin marries Andrette, what example does God's love give for him according to Ephesians 5:25–29?

e. How was Justin and Andrette's relationship a reflection (or not a reflection) of the love of God?

f. Consider 1 John 4:7–12. How could God's love be expressed by the parents when they hear the news?

6. Ministry Application

Design a love outreach ministry to help the:

Poor

Homeless

Elderly

Widows

Orphans

Record your ideas for implementing a marriage enrichment ministry in your church.

Describe effective ways to teach teens about relationships and true love.

7. Personal Application

What shows do you watch where the theme is love?

How does the love portrayed on television compare to the love that the Bible describes?

How does a love for things compete with the love of God?

How can you increase your love for your family, friends, relatives, and neighbors?

CHAPTER FIVE

TELEVISION—Christianity and Food

CASE STUDY

Sister Johnson called to tell her daughter the news—her doctor had diagnosed her with diabetes. She would need her daughter's help to get to the doctor's office once a week for the next month of follow-up appointments. Sister Johnson's husband had firmly repeated that he simply did not feel like going because "he was retired." He hadn't seen a doctor in years and disliked going to the office, even to drop her off and to wait for her.

Sister Johnson's daughter knew that something was wrong with her mother and had insisted on a thorough physical for both her parents. Though she was unable to get her father to go, she was grateful that at least her mother's condition was properly diagnosed. She decided to take her mother to the appointments and to help with the grocery shopping and cooking to start her new diet.

Trying to find substitute foods and ingredients for some of the old family recipes became a bonding experience for the mother and daughter as they began to cook together twice a week. One day after Sister Johnson and her daughter returned home from a shopping trip, they found Sister Johnson's husband slumped in a chair in front of the television. He had suffered a stroke.

BIBLE APPLICATION EXERCISES
God is Our Provider

1. God's Provision for His People

a. How did God provide food for Adam (Genesis 2:8–9)?

____

____

b. How did God use Joseph to provide food for the nation of Egypt (Genesis 41:40–49, 53–57)?

____

____

c. How did God provide food for the Israelites as they journeyed from Egypt? What did He provide (Exodus 16:11)?

d. God's provision of food for the poor is described in laws of the harvest (Exodus 23:22; Leviticus 19:9). What was His plan?

e. God provided food for the priests under the law. What was provided and under what conditions (Leviticus 22:1, 6–7)?

f. What can we summarize about these Old Testament examples of God's provision of food?

2. God's Provision for His Servants

a. How did Jesus instruct His disciples to support themselves when He sent them out to minister in Matthew 10:5–15?

b. What are the consequences for those who support those sent by God, according to Matthew 10:40–42?

c. What are the reasons given by Paul for support of ministers in 1 Corinthians 9:3–14?

d. How are the elders of the church to be treated according to 1 Timothy 5:17–18?

e. In Ezekiel 34:1–10, what warning does God provide to those leaders who are not faithful in their leadership?

f. Is the church today following God's pattern for support of those in ministry? Why or why not?

3. New Testament Teachings on Food and Provision

a. According to Jesus' message recorded in Matthew 6:25–33, what is more important than eating or drinking?

b. Why would God view these as more important than food and clothing?

c. What does Jesus say we should seek instead of worrying about what we will eat or drink?

d. How did Jesus demonstrate God's ability to provide food in Matthew 14:15–21 and 15:32–39?

e. How did Jesus respond to the Pharisees' traditions concerning washing before eating in Matthew 15:1–3, 10–11?

f. Do you think that Sister Johnson's husband will pay more attention to her and his health since suffering a stroke?

4. Feeding Those in Need

Sister Johnson heads the hospitality ministry at her church. Each Thanksgiving they prepare food baskets for about 100 families. This ministry has gone on for nearly 20 years.

a. What is the greatest commandment, and how does this ministry fulfill it (Matthew 22:37–40; Mark 12:28–31)?

b. How might Sister Johnson's ministry be viewed by Jesus, according to Matthew 25:35?

c. In 2 Corinthians 9:9, what promise is made to those who feed the poor?

d. What guidance is given in 2 Thessalonians 3:8–10 about who should be eligible for help from Sister Johnson's ministry?

e. What are some ways to assure that a food ministry is effectively reaching those who are in greatest need (James 2:14–16)?

f. Consider the establishment of the food ministry in Acts 6:1–6. What were some critical steps taken in the formation of this ministry?

5. Food and Care of the Temple (the Body)

a. According to 1 Corinthians 6:19–20, what is the body and to whom does it belong?

b. What general guidance about food is given in the Jewish law (Deuteronomy 14:3)?

c. What are the consequences of overeating according to Proverbs 23:20–21?

d. How did obesity (excessive weight) bring down a king who oppressed the Israelites (Judges 3:14–25)?

e. Why is it important to bring the body under submission to our spiritual goals (1 Corinthians 9:24–27)?

f. In 1 Timothy 4:8, how does Paul's teaching concerning physical training and spiritual development apply to Sister Johnson's situation?

6. Ministry Application

Consider one or more of the projects below for your church:

Identify several local food programs in your area and determine which one might be best implemented by your church.

If your church provides meals or hosts special occasion dinners, have a dietician evaluate the typical menus for health and wellness. Develop alternative menus for church members who have restricted diets.

Contact World Vision and obtain information on "The Famine," the 30-hour fast for hunger awareness that can be implemented by your youth ministry.

7. Personal Application

Evaluate at least 10 food commercials on television. For each commercial, write down the advertising approach used to try to persuade you to buy. Refer to the list in the textbook.

Make a commitment to avoid watching TV while eating.

Make a plan to exercise regularly; be realistic and keep track of your progress until it becomes a habit (at least 30–45 days).

Evaluate your diet, what do you need to change?

Develop a plan to teach your children about healthy eating.

CHAPTER SIX

TELEVISION—Violence and God's Protection

CASE STUDY

Although shootings in schools have been a problem in the United States for many years, the most devastating shootings occurred April 20, 1999, at Columbine High School in Littleton, Colorado. In the brief span of 16 minutes, two students, in a well-planned attack, randomly shot and killed 12 students and one teacher and wounded 21 others. Then the perpetrators of the attack killed themselves, bringing the death toll to 15. The date of the tragedy was the 110th anniversary of Adolf Hitler's birth and was also the day after the fourth-year anniversary of the Oklahoma City bombing and the day after the sixth-year anniversary of the Branch Davidian standoff in Waco, Texas.

The killers planned much more destruction than that which occurred. They had planted bombs in the school cafeteria and carried automatic weapons and ammunition that could have killed all the nearly 500 students there if things had gone as planned.

Several of the students were asked about their belief in God before they were killed by the attackers. At least one of the students has been held up as a martyr for boldly affirming her belief before being killed. Many Christians were inspired by the story of this student who held on to her faith while facing death, and many students became believers in Jesus Christ after hearing of this tragic event and these faithful victims.

BIBLE APPLICATION EXERCISES
God Is Our Protector

1. God's Presence Revealed

How did God reveal His presence to the following people in these Old Testament Scriptures?

a. Abraham (Genesis 22:11–14) ______________________________

b. Jacob (Genesis 32:24–30) ______________________________

c. Moses (Exodus 3:1–6) ______________________________

d. Samuel (1 Samuel 3:1–10) ______________________________

e. Job (Job 38:1–3) ______________________________

f. How is God revealing His presence to people today? How do we see God's presence in the Columbine case study?

2. God's Protection from Violence in the Old Testament

a. What was the basis for God's protection of Noah and his family from destruction (Genesis 6:8)?

b. How did God protect Lot from the destruction of Sodom and Gomorrah (Genesis 19:15–23)?

c. How was David protected from the death sentence Saul had issued for him (1 Samuel 19:1–6)?

d. What are some of the protections of God mentioned in Psalm 91?

e. How will God protect His people according to Psalm 121?

f. In what ways did God protect the Columbine students?

3. God's Protection from Violence in the New Testament

a. How did God protect the infant Jesus (Matthew 2:13–15)?

b. How did Jesus survive the assassination attempt in His hometown of Nazareth (Luke 4:28–30)?

c. Jesus testified in prayer that He had protected all His disciples except which one (John 17:12)?

d. How was Paul protected from the Jews who sought to kill him in Acts 9:23–25?

e. What did the church do when Herod threatened Peter's life? How was Peter protected by God (Acts 12:5–11)?

f. What does 2 Corinthians 4:7–5:1 teach about our response to threats of violence or physical attack?

4. God's Response to Violent Living

a. How was the earth described in Genesis 6:11–13 and what was God's response?

b. How did God respond to the violence in David's life according to 1 Chronicles 28:2–3?

c. God had delivered David and he gave thanks in Psalm 18:48. Describe David's deliverance.

d. What did John the Baptist teach the soldiers in Luke 3:14?

e. What was Jesus' teaching on violence in Matthew 26:52?

f. In light of the events at Columbine and the violence on television, what messages and warnings should the church have for the nation today?

5. Violence and Life in the Spirit

a. How should we understand the struggle against violence in the media according to Ephesians 6:12?

b. What process should be used to take control of the continuing assault on our minds and senses by television violence (2 Corinthians 10:3–6)?

c. What guidance can we give to young people concerning their response to violence in media (Galatians 5:16–21)?

d. What should be the spiritual mind-set of the Christian facing a violent world (Philippians 2:5–8)?

e. How can Christians be prepared to respond with faith in the presence of violence, like the Columbine students responded (1 Peter 3:15–17)?

f. How is Jesus' teaching on violence in Matthew 11:12 reconciled with the Scriptures above? (Be sure to read the verse in other translations, such as the NIV or NLT.)

6. Ministry Application

Develop a position on gun control and firearms laws in your community based on your views as shaped by the Scriptures and the customs of your community.

Consider a firearms safety training initiative for your church. What precautions should be taken by those that have guns in their home?

What steps can be taken to rid your community of illegal weapons and guns? Develop a plan to assist local law enforcement officials in this effort.

7. Personal Application

Do a violence audit of your favorite television programs. How many have excessive violence? List them below. Make a commitment to stop watching them.

Review your children's or relatives' video game collections for violent titles. List them below, and consider destroying them or selling them to game recyclers. Use the proceeds to contribute to a domestic violence shelter or another ministry.

Make a commitment not to watch violent movies. Write your commitment below and include Scripture references to help ground your commitment with biblical truth. Memorize your Scripture(s).

CHAPTER SEVEN

TELEVISION— Hip-Hop and Sin

CASE STUDY

The Passion of the Christ has been the most controversial Christian movie ever produced and the most profitable. This story of the trial and crucifixion of Jesus Christ has been viewed, criticized, praised, analyzed, and even demonized by many since its release. Through its extraordinarily violent and graphic imagery, the movie has forced reactions from believers and nonbelievers as only a movie can.

Much of the criticism of the movie has focused on the Catholic themes of the film and Catholic beliefs of the film's creator. Central to Catholicism is the crucifix—an image of the dead Jesus on the cross. What is less clear from the film is why Jesus died and the fact that He defeated the Cross by rising from the dead. The Resurrection scene is about two minutes of the film.

Phil saw the film and insisted that his girlfriend, Sylvia, go with him to see it a second time. He believed that by taking her to the movie, he could convince her to stop listening to explicit lyric rap music and maybe to join his church. He was convinced that the graphic scenes of the Crucifixion would make her want to know more about Christianity. Sylvia was not persuaded. She felt that her music tastes had nothing to do with her spirituality and that she was basically a good person. In her opinion, she was a better person than many of the people she knew who attended Phil's church, and she never attended R-rated movies like the *The Passion of the Christ*.

BIBLE APPLICATION EXERCISES
Christ Was Crucified

1. God's Word on Sin

a. What was the penalty for sin defined by God in Genesis 2:16–17? ____________________

b. What is the warning against the sin of forgetting the Lord given in Deuteronomy 6:10–15? __________

____

c. What were the consequences of sin and disobedience defined by God in Deuteronomy 28:15–20?

____

____

d. What did Jesus teach concerning the continued validity of the law and its prohibitions against sin in Matthew 5:17–18?

___

___

e. What is the role of the Holy Spirit with regard to sin according to John 16:8–9?

___

___

f. What is the purpose of the law, and what is its relationship to the sin of man (Galatians 3:19–22)?

___

___

2. The Holiness of God

What do the following Scriptures say about the holiness of God?

a. Exodus 15:11 ___

b. Psalm 60:6 ___

c. Isaiah 6:3 ___

d. Psalms 145:17 ___

e. John 17:11b ___

f. Considering the Scriptures above—especially Isaiah 6:3—what should our response be to a Holy God?

___

___

3. Television Promotes Sin

a. What was Jesus' prophecy about the evil to come in Matthew 24:6–8?

___

___

b. How does Paul's description of the last days in 2 Timothy 3:1–7 line up with much of television news and current events today?

___

___

c. What is the teaching of Ephesians 4:22–24 concerning the walk of the believer? How does it compare to the ways of those so often shown on television today?

d. According to Ephesians 5:11, how should the believer respond to the sin on television and in the world today?

e. What is the calling of the believer concerning the evil on television and in the world according to 1 Thessalonians 4:1–7?

f. Considering the Scriptures above and the state of television and movies today, how would you advise Phil on the use of any movie as a witnessing strategy?

4. Sin and "Good" People

Sylvia believes that her goodness may be enough, especially when compared to others. What do the following Scriptures teach about "comparing" your way to heaven?

a. Isaiah 53:6

b. Matthew 5:20

c. Matthew 5:43–48

d. Romans 3:9–18

e. Romans 3:23

f. Galatians 2:16

5. From Sin to Transformation

Use the following Scriptures to develop a plan of action for Phil's witness and ministry to Sylvia:

a. Romans 12:1–2

b. Ephesians 5:15–16

c. Philippians 4:8

d. Colossians 3:2 ______

e. 1 Thessalonians 5:22 ______

f. James 1:13–15

______

______

______

______

6. Ministry Application

Conduct a survey of your church members' television viewing habits. Do the viewing habits of different church groups (Sunday School class, VBS class, auxiliary) relate in any ways to problem areas or sin in your church?

______

______

______

List your favorite TV shows.

______

______

Then list major life problems that you or your friends/family are experiencing. Look for relationships.

______

______

7. Personal Application

How do areas of struggle in your own personal life relate to your viewing habits?

______

______

Are there things that you watch that feed your areas of weakness? Focus your Bible reading around problem areas.

______

______

Develop a personal Bible study around an area of life where you are struggling with sin (James 4:17).

Fast from TV; instead, do your study for a two-week period.

CHAPTER EIGHT

TELEVISION—Life after Death

CASE STUDY

Mother Williams went to the door expecting that her grandson had finally arrived from college. She opened it to find two Jehovah's Witnesses, *Watchtower* magazines in hand, asking if they could come in and do a Bible study. Just as she was about to tell them that John 1:1 was different in her Bible and they needed to go read a real Bible, her grandson walked up. She asked the "witnesses" to excuse her while she let her grandson in. Then she politely smiled, said she was busy now, and then closed the door.

Brandon was visiting his grandmother for spring break and was anxious to tell her about his Comparative Religions class and his study of reincarnation in Eastern religions. He hugged his grandmother and laughed as she told him that she almost let those people in who think the Holy Spirit is nothing more than a force, like electricity. Brandon had heard his grandmother witness to the witnesses many times growing up. He knew that the ideas of the nineteenth century American founder of this group did not line up with the biblical teachings his grandmother raised him to believe. But Brandon wanted to know what his grandmother believed about reincarnation and the other beliefs about what happens at death that he had just learned about. As they sat together and talked, Mother Williams silently prayed that God would lead her to help her grandson to understand the truth of the Resurrection.

BIBLE APPLICATION EXERCISES
Christ Is Risen

1. Mary Encounters the Resurrected Christ

a. What time of day did Mary go to the grave site of Jesus (Matthew 28:1; John 20:1)?

____

____

b. Why was Mary going to the tomb of Jesus (Mark 16:1)?

____

____

c. Who else was with Mary at the tomb (compare Matthew 28:1; Mark 16:1, 9; and Luke 24:10)?

d. What message did Mary first deliver to the disciples, and what was their response (John 20:2–4)?

e. What message was given to Mary by Jesus to deliver to the disciples (John 20:17)?

f. Do the differences in the four Gospel accounts of Mary's encounter affect the truth of the story?

2. The Disciples Encounter the Resurrected Christ

a. Who were the first two disciples to come to the tomb of the resurrected Jesus (John 20:2–4)?

b. What did the disciples observe at the tomb, and what was their response?

c. How did Jesus make His first appearance to the disciples together (John 20:19)?

d. How did Jesus demonstrate to the disciples that He was truly resurrected? What was their response (John 20:20)?

e. What three messages did Jesus give to the disciples in this encounter (John 20:21–22)?

f. How should Mother Williams use the encounter of Jesus to give assurance to Brandon that the Resurrection is a reality?

3. Jesus Appears to Thomas

a. What was the testimony of the disciples to Thomas in John 20:24–25? How did he respond?

b. How long was it before Thomas was again with the disciples when Jesus appeared (John 20:26)?

c. What did Jesus say and do to indicate that this appearance was for the benefit of Thomas (John 20:27)?

d. What was Thomas's testimony after his encounter with Jesus?

f. What was the purpose of the record of these events in John's gospel? How can Brandon use this truth when responding to friends who may question Christ's resurrection?

4. The Resurrected Jesus Christ

a. How many days was Christ bodily on earth after the Resurrection (Acts 1:3)?

b. What actions support the fact that Jesus was resurrected bodily and was not a ghost or an illusion of those who saw Him (Matthew 28:9; Luke 24:36–43; John 20:25–29)?

c. What was Jesus' explanation of the Resurrection to His followers in Luke 24:44–46?

d. What were the circumstances of Jesus' third appearance to the disciples, and who was present (John 21:1–14)?

e. How many people saw Jesus after His resurrection, according to 1 Corinthians 15:6?

f. Summarize the teachings of the passages in the previous questions to use as proof of the resurrection of Christ.

5. Christianity Requires Resurrection

a. How does Paul's writing in 1 Corinthians 15:1–8 seek to prove that the Resurrection was an actual physical occurrence?

b. Why is a belief in the Resurrection so critical for all Christians, according to 1 Corinthians 15:12–14?

c. What connection between Adam and Christ is made in 1 Corinthians 15:21–22?

d. How does Paul make it clear in 1 Corinthians 15:35–38 that we will have our own identity after our resurrection?

e. What are the characteristics of the resurrected body according to 1 Corinthians 15:42–44? How were these characteristics demonstrated by the resurrected Christ?

f. Mother Williams' grandson, Brandon, was taught that reincarnation is the belief held by some Buddhists and Hindus that the soul is purified after death by returning to earth in the form of another body or as an animal depending on the deeds one did in life. How do the teachings of the Resurrection refute these beliefs?

6. Ministry Application

Working with your study group, write a short (15 minutes or less) drama or play about the resurrected Christ. Present the play in your Bible study or Sunday School class as an object lesson that demonstrates the reality of the risen Lord Jesus.

Research the beliefs about life after death held by other faiths. Test your church or class members on these differences.

7. Personal Application

Define your life's purpose.

List your fears about your own death

Write your epitaph/eulogy.

Define in your own words what you will experience after death, and use these Scripture passages to support your description:

I Corinthians 15

I Thessalonians 5:13–18

CHAPTER NINE

TELEVISION—God's People at Worship

CASE STUDY

Sandra felt like her spiritual needs were being met by the weekly Bible study she watched on television, but she longed to reconnect with her twin brother, Leon, in a church service, like they did when they were children. In fact, Sandra had been planning to visit her brother's church for several months, but she just could not get comfortable with the idea. While she was happy her brother had accepted Christ as his Savior, she was not really sure about the church he was attending. She had heard that the praise and worship that began each service sometimes lasted an hour or more. She was even more concerned about the praise dancers. Her girlfriend told her that the outfits they wore were formfitting. Sandra could not imagine what this added to the service.

Her brother Leon was convinced that this church was where he was supposed to be. His work with the church's prison ministry allowed him to do something he had always wanted to do. Since his best friend from high school had gone to prison 10 years ago, he had wondered about just how bad it was in there. Leon's involvement in the prison ministry not only satisfied his curiosity, he felt that God was really using him to bring hope to the lives of men who, like his friend, had lost their way.

BIBLE APPLICATION EXERCISES
The Church at Worship

1. Jesus' Teachings on Worship

a. Who should be the object of worship (John 4:23)? ______________________________

b. What did Jesus teach about worshiping things (Matthew 4:8–10)?

____

____

c. If God is the object of worship, what did Jesus mean in His prayer recorded in John 17:5?

____

____

d. What kind of worshipers does God seek (John 4:23–24)?

e. What did Jesus teach about the appropriate place for worship (John 4:21–24)?

f. Based on the Scriptures above, who do you believe is the true worshiper, Sandra or Leon? Why?

2. Corporate and Private Worship

a. When Solomon built the first temple and all the people were gathered, how did they worship God (1 Chronicles 7:1–3)?

b. What acts of worship took place when the rebuilding projects were completed in Nehemiah 8:1–6?

c. How did Job respond to the deaths of his children and loss of his wealth (Job 1:20)?

d. How did David prepare for worship after the death of his son (2 Samuel 12:19)?

e. How is the worship described in Revelation 4:8–10?

f. Considering the Scriptures above, should Sandra be concerned about the worship at her brother's church?

3. Worship and Praise

Describe the events that resulted in worship and praise in the following Scriptures:

a. 1 Samuel 1:26–28; 2:1–10

b. Judges 4:23–24; Judges 5

c. Daniel 2:1–23

d. Luke 19:37–38

e. Acts 2:43–47

f. How would the hour spent in praise at Leon's church likely compare with the time spent in these scriptural examples?

4. Sacrifice and Worship

How are sacrifice and worship related in the following Scriptures:

a. Genesis 22:1–5

b. Deuteronomy 12:1–14

c. 1 Samuel 1:3

d. 1 Kings 18:20–39

e. 2 Chronicles 29:27–31

f. What does God consider a living sacrifice, according to Romans 12:1–2?

5. Worship and Dance

a. What did the Children of Israel do after God closed the Red Sea on the Egyptian army and saved them (Exodus 15:19–20)?

b. How did the people celebrate the death of Goliath (1 Samuel 18:6)?

c. What was David's response when the ark, which represented the presence of God, was returned to Israel in 2 Samuel 6:14? ______

d. How should we let people praise and worship God, according to Psalm 149:3?

______

______

c. What does Psalm 150:4 command us to do? ______

f. Considering the Scriptures above, how should Leon respond to his sister's concerns about the praise dancers in his church?

______

______

6. Ministry Application

Compare worship in your ministry to the worship experiences in the Bible. Identify five ways that your worship experiences are similar or different from these biblical models.

______

______

What considerations should be made for change or alteration of your corporate worship?

______

______

7. Personal Application

In what ways should you change your personal worship experiences in light of the examples in Scripture?

______

______

Commit to elevating your private worship experience. What changes do you believe you need to make?

______

______

CHAPTER TEN

TELEVISION—The World of Reality

CASE STUDY

Tom Skinner spent his life in ministry with a focus on developing the spiritual potential of others. Like Barnabas in the Bible, Tom was an encourager who was not willing to see anyone left behind. Ordained at 17 by the United Missionary Baptist Association of Greater New York, Tom formed the Harlem Evangelistic Association and began to hold meetings and crusades in New York, the Caribbean, and in cities around the country. Later named Tom Skinner Associates, his organization's programs expanded to include ministry to high school and college students, motivational seminars, and community development projects. A learning center started in Newark, New Jersey provided computer training and spiritual and vocational guidance for inner-city youth.

Tom often worked with prominent White evangelists, such as Billy Graham and was one of the participants in the formation of the Association of Black Evangelicals. He was a persistent critic of racism in America and served as a positive force for developing young Black Christian leaders. Tom provided a bridge between the Black and White evangelical communities and published books that challenged both groups to live according to a kingdom mandate. Tom worked as a mentor and chaplain for several professional athletes and sports teams and was one of the earliest people to develop this ministry outreach. Throughout the 1970s and 1980s, he served as team chaplain for the Washington Redskins. Just before his death in 1994, Tom moved from New York to the Washington, D.C. area where he started the Skinner Farm Leadership Institute. Through Tom's efforts and inspiration, today many other organizations continue reaching and encouraging people with the Gospel of the kingdom.

BIBLE APPLICATION EXERCISES
Living As a Christian

1. Putting Your Money Where Your Faith Is

a. What does Jesus command that we do with our treasures (Matthew 6:19–21)?

____

____

b. In Matthew 19:16–22, how and why did the rich young ruler respond to this teaching?

c. What was Jesus' promise for those who sacrificed for the kingdom (Mark 10:28–30)?

d. What principle of giving is shared by Jesus in Luke 6:38?

e. Why are we challenged to make a choice about the values of television and contemporary society and those things that are important to God (Matthew 6:24)?

f. Why would Tom Skinner—with his college education, leadership skills, and determination—choose a life in ministry instead of some other path? What critical choices are involved in a decision of this type?

2. Bringing Thoughts into Obedience

a. Television has become the constant companion for many. What does the Bible say the effect will be (1 Corinthians 15:33)?

b. Advertisers spend billions of dollars to change the hearts and minds of television viewers. What does the Bible say about it (Proverbs 23:7)?

c. What is the nature of this battle that makes it especially important to guard our thought life 2 Corinthians 10:3–5)?

d. Considering the previous Scriptures, what is the strategy for resisting the attack on our minds (2 Corinthians 10:5)?

e. Instead of the negative things on television, what does the Bible say that we should be thinking about (Philippians 4:8)?

f. Tom's life shows that he was able to focus his mind on the things of God. What were some of the events of the 1960s and 1970s that could have distracted him?

3. Loving God

a. What are the results of a heart that feeds on the love of God as opposed to the love of the world and the negative images of television (Luke 6:45)?

b. What evidence shows that someone loves God (John 14:15)?

c. What evidence shows that someone does not love God (John 14:24)?

d. What was Jesus' command concerning the love of God (Matthew 22:37b–38)?

e. How will God respond to those who demonstrate their love for Him (John 14:23)?

f. What evidence was there in Tom Skinner's life that indicated that he loved God?

4. Loving Your Neighbor

a. A personal relationship with God is important; but is that enough (Matthew 22:39)?

b. What was Jesus' response when asked the question, "Who is my neighbor" (Luke 10:29–37)?

c. Do "neighbors" have to be friends of yours to be loved (Luke 6:32–36)?

d. What is God's response to the one who loves others in the way God commands (Luke 6:32–36)?

e. What is God's response to those who refuse to love according to His standard (Matthew 25:31–46)?

f. Identify the ways Tom Skinner showed love for his neighbors.

5. Leading People to Christ

a. What was Jesus' last commandment in Matthew 28:19?

b. What should we teach those who we lead to Christ (Matthew 28:20)?

c. Where should we go to witness to and seek to lead people to Christ (Acts 1:8)?

d. Is it solely the responsibility of leaders like Tom Skinner or can average people be used to lead people to Christ?

e. Is praying for the lost enough (Romans 10:14–17)?

f. Tom Skinner led many to Christ even though he was not a movie or television celebrity. How could television have been used effectively to enhance his ministry?

6. Ministry Application

Define a new ministry for your neighborhood.

Identify needs

Assess current ministries

Select a new ministry for an area of unmet need

Define goals/objectives (what we hope to achieve)

Develop strategies (how we will get it done)

Determine tactics (time, events, and responsibilities)

List resource requirements (budgets and cash requirements)

7. Personal Application

List some people that God has placed in your path in the following categories:

Friends

Family

Coworkers

Define a ministry for each that you can fulfill. Think of the several ways that Barnabas lived the Christian life as you formulate your answers.

NOTES